The Assay

Acknowledgments

Many thanks to the editors of the following, in which some of
these poems and translations first appeared:

Areté, *The Food Programme* (BBC Radio 4), *Brittle Star, Cimarron
Review* and *Cumberland Poetry Review* (USA), *Dimui Review*
and *Jerusalem Review* (Israel), *European Judaism*, *The Interpreter's
House*, *The Jewish Quarterly*, *Jewish Renaissance*, *The London
Magazine*, *Magma*, *Modern Poetry In Translation*, *The North*, *PEN
International*, *Petits Propos Culinaires*, *PN Review*, *Poetry Review*,
Sameach, *Second Light*, *The Sephardi Bulletin*, *The Wolf*. 'Knitting'
was commissioned by the Poetry Society and appears on their web-
site at poetrysociety.org.uk/content/knit/week3.

The poems in the section 'And for Years After' were written for
JWA Women's Shelter

The Assay
Yvonne Green

Smith/Doorstop Books

Published 2010 by
Smith/Doorstop Books
The Poetry Business
Bank Street Arts
32-40 Bank Street
Sheffield S1 2DS
www.poetrybusiness.co.uk

ISBN 978-1-906613-17-4

British Library Cataloguing-in-Publication Data.
A catalogue record for this book is available from the
British Library.

Typeset by Utter
Printed by MPG Biddles Ltd., King's Lynn, Norfolk
Cover design by Utter

Smith/Doorstop Books is a member of Inpress,
www.inpressbooks.co.uk. Distributed by Central Books Ltd.,
99 Wallis Road, London E9 5LN.

The Poetry Business gratefully acknowledges the help of
Arts Council England.

Supported by
ARTS COUNCIL
ENGLAND

CONTENTS

Translations
from the Russian of Semyon Lipkin
(1911-2003)

*for my parents, Vicky (née Ribacoff) and Charles Mammon
with love*

I
Boukhara

SOURIYA

'My mother told me a long time ago
you can eat a mountain of salt with someone
and still you cannot know them.

I lived with Moshiach and Souriya
together in one house for forty years,
Mirka and I raised our daughters with them.

At our table we did not eat a mountain of salt.
Together we ate maybe this much.'
His hands and his mind's eye reckoned out

a mound from his belly to his chin.
'So how could I know what she would do to me?'

BASMATI

I don't measure the rice
I wash it in an ancient sieve
using my palm and the tips
of my fingers stroking towards
my belly and up and
then brushing away with
the back of my fingers, the rice
a caress on the knuckles
and a satisfying gravel
on the flat of my hand
the cold water cooling
my pulse like eau de cologne
the suggestion of fragrance
promising from the lifeless
wetting grains

my left hand dreaming
on the sieve handle
shuffling the sieve
like a wallah working a fan
the metal strips
of the handle loop pressed into
my dry palm
two different rhythms one dry and hard
and one too cold now
and lively with rice back and forth
back and forth

OUR FOOD

The smell of rice cooking is the smell of my childhood
and a house devoid of cooking smells is no home.
Sometimes I visited other houses which smelled like our house
heavy with the steaming of mint or dill
and tiny cubes of seared liver all seeping into rice,
which would become green and which was called *bachsh*.

We felt foreign, shy of our differentness
unable to explain the sweetness of brown rice called *osh sevo*,
where prunes and cinnamon and shin meat had baked slowly
melting into the grains of rice which never lost their form.
Our eggs, called *tchumi osh sevo*, were placed in water
with an onion skin and left to coddle overnight
so that their shells looked like dark caramel
their flesh like café au lait.

Our salad was chopped,
a woman appraised her refinement by how fast
and how finely she could chop cucumbers, onions, parsley,
coriander and trickiest of all tomatoes 'no collapsed tomatoes'
a young girl would be scolded if she tried to get her efforts
into the large bowl that she and her mother
(and the other women, if there were a party) were filling.

The knife scraped across the raised chopping board,
always away from the body in a sweeping gesture.
The combination of ingredients never measured
other than by eye. Salt, pepper and lemon, vinegar
or Sabbath wine added at the last moment
so that this *slota* should not be *asalak* – mushy.

JOMA

Unevenly edged, cream, indigo, orange and aquamarine oblongs,
parallel against a coral background. Long wide cuffs and hems
brocaded with plum, yellow, turquoise and sapphire chevrons.
No two *joma* are the same. These came from Boukhara.

When stored they're turned inside out by hands in arm holes,
then turned inward by hands back to back.
Then the great weight of silk is rolled by one hand over the other
the thickness pressed under the right elbow and wrapped in muslin
which absorbs the scent in the grosgrain but not the colour from the *ikat*.

We dance at weddings, with them around our shoulders
our backs straight, elbows bent, hands raised, wrists rotating
then we drape them around someone else, miming an invitation
to follow the old ways. On Pesach, we come to a table
vivid with stacks of romaine lettuce, and clouds of salty water
wearing my grandparents' gestures in ceremonial coats
which carry the musk of generations, of free men.

DOYRA

Shallow, like a big tambourine, without jingles,
its thick cream parchment fixed to its dark
wood hoop by round headed brass tacks. Yula
first warmed its surface with a candle flame.

Then he raised and lowered the drum time and time
again, balancing it on his palms, as though to estimate
its weight, to offer it to the Almighty, or to create suspense
in the company, who talked and sucked their teeth, seat-backs
to the walls, appetites sated, the rice, the fruits, the tea things,
gone back to the kitchen.

Suddenly, as if mid-phrase, the balls and tips
of his fingers began to produce a deep, loud,
repetitive rhythm, the company kept up their chat
but lowered their tone. He sang, like a sigh, again
and again, until he was joined by someone, insistent,
in a higher key.

This was an engagement, there would be no dancing,
Yula's ritual stopped, as abruptly as it began, he stowed
the *doyra* behind his chair. The fiancés, seated slightly
apart, inclined for a photograph, until their foreheads
touched, then everyone shouted *gorki*, and they kissed,
supposedly for the first time.

TAKING THE BRIDE TO THE HENNA NIGHT

You sat in the evening light, shawled in gold and cream
and white. Your hair which you try so hard to tame
with unguents, was playing around your face
like tendrils of amber. You caught the late sunshine
in your eyes, in the milk of your skin, in your curls.
Then you caught the late sunshine on your swaddling silks
and it reflected into the glow of you, which in turn
created a pointillism of radiance. Who would ever believe
that a London taxi cab could contain such a moment?

. . .

Last night we dressed in the the silks of the orient, we rang
bells and banged cymbals and screamed into the dark.
Last night we ululated with ecstasy and we reflected
on our marriages, on our babies, on our mothers.
Last night we met like women in a harem and my mother
said she envied her friends who were widowed with a hefty inheritance.

. . .

It was a night when silks flew, whirling with their wearers,
glistening with real gold threads in creamy whites.
It was a night when girls were to become women
and when women recaptured girlhood. The septuagenarians
danced like houris and showed the virgins how to please a man
and the virgins danced without understanding radiant in their innocence.

. . .

It was twilight in that room, like an unlit bedroom at dusk,
spirits darted, darted and glittered. It was a room full of pasts
and presences, it was a room where a future was being invited,
like an honoured guest. It was a room where a future was being ignited.

BOUKHARIAN BOYS

Gold skinned youths powered forward
shoulder to shoulder, sternum raised
and danced holding each others' backs
like Greeks. They dipped low in concert
then they reached up as one; glorying
in their bodies, they swooped, tumbled
somersaulted together like Kenyan boys
then spun away like dervishes.

Caught by drums, they glanced at one another
synchronising a tribute to the seated newlyweds.
Then a block of thick-set fathers, grandfathers
and a great-grandfather, moved forward
shoulder to shoulder, greyed heads erect
suit jackets fastened, raised hands cupped
they swayed left and right and the panting boys
stood back and clapped time.

BIVI

Bivi had a round white face
and a reputation for being tough.
Her shiny nose dripped.

She was fat and shuffled,
she even had fat feet
stuffed into her shoes.

She moved about the kitchen
without losing her temper.
She could do lots of things we couldn't

like she kept a live fish in the bath
after she bought it on Friday
and then killed it dead.

She offended people in her family
and terrified them with one look.
But my Dad, and her other surviving son
softly called her *maman*.

Sometimes her eyes looked nowhere
and her face got thin and even whiter.
If she saw me noticing
she put a stop to that.

JOMI HAMMAM

After a hot soak and a sit in the steam which she trapped
keeping the bathroom door tightly shut, *Bivi* would wrap me
in more than one towel then she gave me a jomi hammam
which was red, blue and white and trailed like a giant's coat.
She tied the belt around me twice and turbaned my head,
then put me under a feather *corpa* to wait, 'not to catch cold'.

It felt nice, weighted down with all that prohibition, safe
from the danger of – well I wasn't sure what. Today I bathe,
sit tight in warm towels and wait, but they don't feel like Bivi's
and I'm never sure when it's safe to emerge.

AZZAZEL

Pinchas Mammon *rachmat koonah*
was unusually tall for a Boukharian boy
and his parents' only son.

He was never allowed to leave the house
unless a servant walked in front of him
and led a goat to deflect the evil eye.

Boukharian women never went out,
they were born and died at home,
on their wedding days they were taken
to live at their mother-in-laws' houses.
They made the journey in a curtained litter.

DHIMMI

Dhimmi under Sharia Law says Jew or Christian *gav neza*, don't speak.
Dhimmi says *mekusham*, be careful. Dhimmi says *dar a bah*, close the door.
Dhimmi says, even inside be on guard. Dhimmi's Boukharian grandchild
can teach Europe how faster to bend the knee. I forgot in your schools, but
now I am reminded. Build your house lower than a Moslem's. Wear yellow
raiment. Hang a cloth from your window to identify your home. If you get
hit or insulted by a Moslem say thank you. Don't ride a camel or a horse but
an ass or a donkey and dismount if a Moslem approaches, for you are less
than the *khar*, beast of burden. If a Moslem approaches step off the
pavement, lower your eyes and bend your back before him. Dhimmi says you
may not bear witness against a Moslem, you must guard against any deroga-
tion from Islam and be prepared for a beating as you pay your tax for
protection. Dhimmi says contain women, hide aspiration and wealth.
Reprise conversation with hamdellella, if Allah wills it and mashalla, thanks
to Allah's will. Dhimmi says move as one, pray as one, think as one.
Dhimmi says you must leave your face in the mirror of your protector's
sect, you must think about inner or actual conversion, forced or pragmatic.
Dhimmi says you must infantalise your household and protect it with rubric.

BINYAMIN

Mammon was taken
at 12 years old
and converted to Islam
for a woman without
a son. His mother saw
the walls of the house
where he was raised,
from her own roof.
She saw him walking
outside in the street
but there was nothing
she could do. *Toba
karam*, pity her.

In every generation
we call one boy
Binyamin Katan
Baer Binyamin
Baruch Binyamin.
Adding something
to his name to change
his luck.

MEAL TIMES

They never spoke except to each other.
Love was shown through food
through the soup in our bowls,
unlaid chicken eggs the golden prizes,
neck bone and skin, the careless gestures,
vermicelli measured out as praise.

'Silence while we eat.' A piercing eye.
The aunts, the mothers, older sisters
were in charge of everything. To the men
we were invisible. But we feared them
as they disappeared huge mounds of rice
from long oval dishes, as they opened
their mouths over bones and crushed them
with gold teeth like the raisins in *pilaf sofi*
as they talked as though they were arguing
as they laughed as though they were crying
as they enforced taboos which were never named.
Waste was a sin and the task set out on our plates
was impossible.

THERE'S A DIFFERENT HISTORY

There's a different history to the tarmac streets and traffic lights,
it's a stark landscape, where turquoise minarets break the dark
and where the mind's eye sees food and raiment and men
leaving and returning with buttoned lips, released
in the intensity of the household, salved on the *corpa*,
bed of eiderdowns, unending goose down, rising
with each pat of the hand, with each head thrown back,
on the *bolish*, pillow, releasing a sparse snow,
which tickled my nostrils and made me wheeze, countries later.

There is a different story to cold knees and baked beans.
Women moving monolithically from *deg i choya*, cast iron
cooking pots, to *lingharie*, huge oval dishes peaked with rice,
brown rice, green rice, rice oranged with carrot slivers, *lingharie*
held on flat palms, fingers spread, brought to the table triumphantly,
the left hand sliding the dish noiselessly onto the table
bsiri man from my soul.

There is no outside really, in my story, there is only *choy covot*,
green tea, in a small bowl, held against my grandmother's temple,
a piece of sugar between her eye teeth. There is only the anticipation
of the meal and after the meal and women working and men talking,
arguing and then talking again. There are *luvs*, diamonds of marzipan
covered in chopped pistachios, I lick the top off mine.
No one ever describes the outside
their minds cordoned by the seamless family.
Ama, your paternal aunt, was depressed at this time of year too.
We never ate dairy products in Boukhara.
Havoney for a child to speak that way to his *modar*.

There is a different language which has a word for older sister, *apa*,
younger sister, maternal aunt but no word for astronaut. Once I wrote
a dictionary of its words, *Alephi osh*, coriander, *badvachta*, poor thing,
coporoytisheva, let me be sacrificed to save you from harm.
So we ate so we loved.

THE PARENTS

It's good to have you to stay
in your extreme old age
finally, all to myself
and you can't go off anywhere
or rather you need me
as you keep wanting to go places

I'm glad to take you.
I enjoy listening,
watching, keeping you happy.

You don't listen to me
nothing changes there
but you do to the children.

Is it our custom
that grandparents hear
and parents must be deaf?

I've lost our language,
our un-named behaviours persist
bewilder, estrange us from others.

I want you to explain it to me
or at least the part you understand,
but you smile at familiar meals
and as ever leave my questions
half-answered.

KHUNDAL KHON

was my great great aunt, a poet, who declaimed
in the Court of the Emir of Boukhara. Not a concubine
(she married in her time and went to live in Jerusalem)
but his solace, she would stand and recite, all day long.

A commentator, a weigher of words, a Jewess
with the ear of the Moslem potentate, whose command
was absolute and whose subjects deferred in every regard.
Did she flatter him, did she offer insights, was she veiled?

II
And For Years After

THAT I MAY KNOW YOU

Let me visit your house
and eat something
of what is on your table
hear you and know
some of your language

Fear those of our
differences which I
am aware of, walk
barefoot, listening
for the steadiness
of breath

AMNESIA

My mother also got amnesia about hitting us
she smiled, *I still remember being pinched*
until my mouth opened. I understand it now,
if I didn't eat – I'd die.
With my father it was different,
he just needed to take off his belt
and we all ran. She raised her eyes and laughed.
I barely knew her but I could see the bedroom
dark with Austrian furniture.

WALKING THE BOYS TO SCHOOL

in her low brimmed hat, her eyes dull,
her mind confused, her children silent,
they've learnt to be silent
after the whisky on the Sunday night table.
She kids herself they've never seen,
sends them to bed at the first signs.
Next week she'll invite family,
at least he'll wait 'til they're gone
or sleep early and plead work pressure
for which he'll be forgiven, he's always forgiven.

Walking the boys to school in her low brimmed hat
her eyes dull, her whole world in this day,
in these children, in this home, in this community,
in this man. She lifts her face and prays for release,
for the Almighty to restore her value.
She is composed when she walks into school,
she is invisible.

THE FIRST TIME

Came as a shock
his hard hand
swung against
my face
the backs of
my thighs
and deep
into my pride

I thought I was
defiant, separated
from this indignity
haughty
with its perpetrator

when my husband
did it, memories
of my father meant
I was meeting
something familiar
something harder
to escape from
the second time round.

SOMEONE ELSE'S STORY

Riding high
on the crest of the day
doing her work,
feeling the way she does
when she's being her.

Then the phone rings
and it's him
hissing her name
and telling her
that she's nothing

and that he's waiting
for when she gets home
to remind her
what she really is
and she believes him

putting down the phone
and steadying herself.
She does her work quietly
then runs home to him
to be told.

I DIDN'T REALLY REALISE

what was happening
we were both so upset and sorry
so constantly re-starting
clutching at each other
passionate for the clean slate
for the *it will never happen again*.
I provoked him every time,
I kicked myself with it
I never knew when to leave off.
He'd been such a good son
and was a loving father
it was just me
that brought it out in him
his foot his shoe on my back
my hair in his hand
so I thought I'd be bald,
but he never left any marks
that weren't under my clothes
and as I cried he said *come on*
we can get over this or wept
what have I done? Or spat
you bitch watch yourself in future

WE SPEAK ENGLISH NOW

and gratefully. There's been time to read
and work and break bread together,
to translate ourselves, give ourselves strength
for what comes next. Some of us have disappeared
where we best match. Others remain distinct.
Our minds are peppered with our culture
our children's minds with what they've met.
Can new life be complete without old stories,
are there different ways to live?

KAREN'S STORY

Karen snorted cocaine you gave her
had an abortion you paid for
committed suicide when you left her.

In your parents' home you'd seen
Dexedrine and Valium.
A woman ran naked in your garden
as you peeped out at bedtime.
News of her death confused you.
But on Karen's last night
you cried as you told your wife
who was suckling your newborn.

AND FOR YEARS AFTER

you're free and loved
you'll recognise the victim
who says *I cause it...*
my problem is...
or whose children
show the fear
she thinks she's hiding.
And for years after
when you're free
giving love not lip-service
you'll know your worth
your heart and how to prove hope
to the victim. You'll whisper
as you hold her *you're safe now*
your hands can mould your future
if you take them away from your face.

I AM NOT A MOTHER

who fries an onion and fills the house
with expectation, the ever-open presence
alert for returning minions. I am not
the stalwart who never flinches.
I remember my own mother cooking
for everyone, then lying in a dark room.

III
The Assay

GHETTO BLASTER

1962, if not later.
He had a black radio.
He carried it in his arms
but it was supposed to sit
on the sideboard.

He carried it because of
the reception and the reception
made him very angry,
Bordel de bordel de bordel.

We sat at the kitchen table,
having dinner time.
He pressed his ear
to the black fabric speaker.
Static cut at us
above the *actualités*
and I couldn't swallow food.

Years later I saw footage
of how people listened
to the news during The War,
drawn up close to the radio
with frozen expressions.

Now he's 80
and puts CNN on,
loud, over and over again.
Things are important
and require his full attention.

CAR KEYS

She left a good white envelope
with *car keys* scrawled on it,
as if she weren't grown up yet.

She phones me full of her new life,
her new friends. Then she draws breath
and confesses she's cut her long hair,
which had been like shined cinnamon sticks.

Now she'll look like stylish women look.
My girl, whose shoulders used to hunch,
whose eyes would raise and who giggled
if you tried to *posh her up*.

A TRIAL

A trial takes over our lives,
the sequence of questions,
how best to set up a point, bristles
like a horsehair wig under the fingers.
The immediacy terrifies and thrills.

Facts of the case, legal argument
the ground to be laid and relaid in response
to the parties, the witnesses, the advocates, the judge.
A trial confounds expectation.

Work in Chambers has a stately calm, instructions,
clients, the huge table piled with paper and tea cups,
questions and Counsel's advice.

But a trial takes over our lives. You eat quickly
and bless me for telling the bedtime stories,
depend on me for stillness. At night
each of us chips our work from stony silence.

THE PRAYER

We enjoyed these children didn't we,
coaxed them along miles of English sands,
got Bert to dip his feet in rock pools,
watched Rachael love the sea her brother hated.
We both climbed sandbanks, pushed nappied bottoms
over the top and shrieked as we all slid down;
we ate endless fish and chips with ketchupped fingers
and watched them lard their hair, each other and us.
We both bathed them laughing as they bailed water
out of the bath, loving their naked bodies
as they slithered away from our towels.

You like me loved the trip to school,
smiles stolen in the rear-view mirror
and leant into with a turn-around at traffic lights.
If I wave Bert says it's safer to drive with two hands.

We enjoyed these children together,
so we'll both remember
when their bodies move like adults
and when we wait to catch their eyes
as eagerly as they now wait to catch ours.

SNAKES AND WHIPS

I lay cradled, watching
you chauffeur the punt.
The Cherwell was dotted
with pond weed and seeded
with diamonds of light.
We slid over an unbreaking surface,
the children laughed their heads off
as you knelt for overhanging trees,
your eyes wide
as you pointed the top of the pole
like a torch before its length
disappeared into the river.
Snakes and whips Bert said
and you ducked
as the black branches
of a dead willow
passed over us.

COL & GIL

When he spoke he used her name often,
each time as if he were introducing
an interesting person's view or perspective.

His huge face was tight in its shiny skin,
broken veins rilled his cheek bones and nose
as though his life force were breaking through
the mould in which the years had baked his smile.

THE ASSAY

His hammer smashed items
which were going to the melt.
Gutted fob watches,
unhinged cigarette cases,
coffee pots stripped of solder
jangled in old mail bags
because of the high price of silver.
Sometimes there'd be silence
and I'd hear, 'I need to *taste* that.'

I watched as he droppered acid
like a condiment onto an entrée dish
or an epergne expecting his gold incisor
to bite down, while his gigantic hands
held the (as yet intact) antique like a sandwich.

I AM LIVID

because I want him
to begin his holiday
by taking me in his arms
and covering me with attention.

I want him to take me
somewhere temperate
where my skin can feel itself
in the air. I want to lie
and look at nature interrupted

only by opulence and ministrations.
I want to surrender to white sheets
and afternoon siestas, to wake at dusk
to cool water and a silk dress.

To walk into the evening
impeded only by the slightest breeze
and his hand on my waist. I am livid
because he melts for the babies

as I know he would melt for me
if he and I were alone.

It is time.

THERE IS A BOAT

There is a boat I've seen before
I've sailed in it or been told
of dark disabled seas which rend
the clothes and hook the conscious
which take the walking in the square
with handles of a bag crossed
one girl holding each and feeling
the scratch of a struggling hen
on the pink of her legs on the spirit
of her tender years laughing
laughing for years into the future
girls again that day they took
the hen to the slaughter with never
a description of the journey home
the bag must have been heavier
and there would have been a different smell

There's crew on the boat
crew in whites and nods
my plate is decorated
with fish bones and parsley
the sea spray the sea speaking
what we know and we make no move
confused our crew look different now
not ashamed still crisp their arms
still busied relieved of the excuse

A boy walks naked
with the sun and his salopettes
reminding him of his skin
his feet feeling the grass
on soles as pink as a puppy's
his lips smoking a hard reed
rolling it saving its suck

I know you'll say we saw and took action
and that we saw nothing but the white
of uniforms pressed or that we and they
stepped forward and backward
and sat down and stood up
cried laughed ran waited
caused it didn't deserve it
were powerful had no influence
were victims were perpetrators
lived among you were never seen
took were too visible integrated
legitimated illegitimated
were the object of envy admiration
disgust confusion

The wind vomits up black spray
and stings my arms where the fine hairs
grow black in large follicles
I'm eating salt without noticing
but my forearms notice
the sea turns red and this time
I look for words

IV
Originating Summons

THE OBOULE IN ALEXANDRIA CIRCA 1935

Tuesday was my grandmother's day. She would dress and then receive visitors from about ten o'clock. The living room was full of dishes of nuts, long pale raisins and small cakes: *ghorayeba*, as soft as fudge; *conafa*, drizzled with syrup; *baklava*, rice paper cakes interleaved with sugared nuts drenched in rosewater. There were jugs of lemonade, clinking with ice, chipped from huge blocks, delivered, for twelve piastres, to refrigerate the larder. A morning breeze visited, as the ladies sat on the white verandas that encircled the apartment, ornamenting the hour with their commentary. Alexandria's *croisette* lay beneath them, as they were offered different delicacies: *rosquette*, savoury biscuit rings finished with white sesame seeds; cheese or spinach *samosas. Quelques fruits?* At lunch time, a buffet of salads and fish and rice would be laid. Ladies came and went, partook of refreshments joined groups mid-story and left at will. English, French, Italian, Arabic, Greek Boukharian, Hebrew, Russian, Spanish, Ladino were spoken interchangeably and anyone, adult or child who couldn't manage wit, in at least three languages, was seen as deficient. Interaction and grace were as essential as food. In the evening the men arrived and drank whisky. A buffet including meat and chicken would be laid and everyone would help themselves. After the fruits and cakes would come out again with *halawa*, and *luvs*, lemon tea in glasses and green tea in small china bowls. The men would smoke cigars and the children would long ago have licked their fingers in the kitchen and gone to bed. On other days my grandmother attended *the oboule* at someone else's house and was joined by my grandfather at dusk.

MY FATHER'S ROOM

My father had an attic room where he *did his books*
and when he wasn't there I used to go and look.
There were scraps of paper torn off spiral pads;
auction house catalogues, text circled, pages dog eared,
reserve prices marked in code; a hard folding chair;
a splintered trestle table, and always the smell of him.

Next to his room was a room full of books and bookcases;
books in them, on them and on the floor (my dictionary
a tiny *Larousse* covered in brown paper was my father's
after Gurs).

I never sat in the book room when my father was there,
I was afraid of him and anyway we weren't allowed
when he was *concentrating*. He hated *doing his books*
but I think he liked being alone. I'd visit after he'd gone
as a way to be near him. Then I went to the book room
where so many abandoned stories gathered dust
until I opened them, powdering the tips of my fingers.

TRANSGRESSION

At dusk, a veiled woman in a *jellabeya*
comes from the neighbouring Arab village
unwinds her black outerclothes and reveals
trainers and a tracksuit underneath.

Early middle-aged she neatly folds
what looks like her shadow into a backpack
which she fastens and shoulders before jogging
through the streets of *Kokhav Ya-Ir*.

GEORGE'S CABBELDY HOUSE

Our house faced the wind,
was the last one on the mountain,
in a bad state, no one local would live in it,
or take an interest in us until one night
the simple shepherd son of the old couple
from the lower farm went missing
and weather was on the way.
Men fanned across the mountain,
my Val kept the kettle boiling
and nailed a red sweater to the front gate.

By morning all our bacon and bread
was in the stomachs out searching.
It was me who found him, singing
to his sheep. He didn't even know
he was lost. I asked him if he'd like
a cup of tea and something to eat.
He nodded and put his hand to his head,
felt his cap wasn't there and went to get it
from where it had lain under him.
We walked downhill together with his sheep.
The search party nodded at me and left;
the red jersey was gone before we got to Val.

LAG B'OMER

We sifted our sadness
into an *omer* of flour
winnowed white
portioned perpetual
ground but not to talcum.
A coarse meal we offered up,
it's thirty three days since Passover.
Four weeks and five days conspire
to make us play, sing,
have haircuts, light bonfires.

VIGIL

Death, when it came, was a matter
of your right collar bone being suddenly still.
For some time there'd been long gaps
between each of your shallow breaths,
so I wasn't sure if your sons had noticed.
They'd flanked you for hours,
each holding one of your hands,
like children out shopping.
Calling to you *mumsel, mama, mumsel, mama*.
Then your eldest son looked forlorn,
as though he'd been left behind
or lost and he said, *it's over*.

ORIGINATING SUMMONS

Where will you find me if I cannot find myself?
By a name, a strand of hair, the dullness of my eye?
I am locked in a cycle of customs without names,
I marry from a circle that calls me with silence,
that fathers my future and deepens its oblivion.

Why do you want me? Why do I want to be found?
I am unnoticed and the trammels of my footsteps
have comforted my generations. I breathe quietly,
I tread slowly, I work carefully. Will my spine straighten
in the unshuttered light of Israel?

KNITTING

A thought forms in my right fist
until my thumb and little finger stretch
to make the beat of a line.
But then I see my mother's hand
as she put down her knitting,
half-closed her left eye
and walked her thumb and little finger
across my girl's chest.
She never used a pattern or explained,
and suddenly there was a garment.

MOTHER ME ALWAYS

A memory full of senses,
your smell your flesh against my cheek,
your glance which checks my action
your voice I overhear as you deal with others
more lightly than you deal with me.
Mother me always serious, funny, overwrought,
fumbling, certain, prescient, frustrating.
Mother me always with your wisdom
expectation and demands, with being
with your having been.

THE CEMETERY AT ST MARTIN, MAURITIUS

And here bounded by a low wall,
one hundred and twenty-seven gravestones.
All but one died in detention
from nineteen forty-one to nineteen forty-five.

The dead were thirty-five to sixty,
except for two children aged nine and eleven.
I wonder about the very young and the very old,
did they die before their boat docked?

The dead, mainly Viennese, rerouted from Palestine
to Mauritius, from one British protectorate to another,
one hundred and twenty six died of typhus, cholera
and starvation.

WITHOUT YOUR JEWS

or when they lived among you in secret, it was as if
zmirot were unsung, minyanim were ungathered, smachot were silent,
rites of death unobserved. As if kashrut was extinct, mikvah unused.
Chagim were voided, the scent of shabbat disappeared, of havdallah
was never released. The fasts eaten, the feasts starved, learning forgotten,
knowledge feared. It was as if a person had two faces or no face
or as if his child didn't know its own smile,
                his wife didn't speak her own prayers.
Yes, there was commerce and medicine and loyalty and fear.
conversion and reversion and service in language other than their own.
But your Jews were gone or hidden. Hostages of darkened reason
which believes calumny and cannot see what makes a human being.
Which cannot listen or watch or ask questions or make a judgment,
which doesn't know its history and doesn't want to,
doesn't stop with history and doesn't want to.

Without your Jews, or when they lived among you in secret,
communities dismantled, charity abandoned, synagogues emptied,
                schools silenced,
cemeteries unvisited and discourse replaced with whispers.
                Protagonists bared their heads
and changed their names. Blind eyes turned from truth
                unspoken and prevailed.
But you broke the silence of your conversos living in Chancery Lane,
when you let their Dutch, Spanish and Portuguese brethren come back,
some with the old ways and others who had forgotten.
The welcome of your hand will be their testament. The candles
we burn here are your legacy. The beseeching of our prayers
are the inheritance of *the commonweal*.

TO MORDECHAI

After the Hebrew of chapter four of The Book of Esther

You told me never to say who I was
but now you mourn at the Palace gates
call to our ancestors, lie in sackcloth
ignore protocol and pray in Hebrew.
Your grief cuts the peace,
it's on the breeze, in the fountains
it chokes me.
Wear the robes I send you, it's safer.

Why didn't you wear them,
why are you still crying, leaving me hollow?
You raised me, I'm afraid without you.
Tell Hasach my chamberlain
when he comes to the City Square,
don't leave me without news,
don't make me ask again.

Hasach showed me the poster
of the royal decree,
the killings won't start for a year.
Xerxes hasn't called me in thirty days
if I go to him I could die now,
shouldn't I wait 'til he calls me?
There's still time.

You say I must speak now,
that this may be why I was taken from you
and brought to The Palace. You say hurry.
Then tell Shushan's Jews to pray
and fast with me for three days.
I'll visit the king with bloodless lips
and parched with prayer I'll speak out.

Translations from the Russian
of *Semyon Lipkin* (1911-2003)

CHARRED

and ashen I whisper *I've been cremated*
in deserted barracks on Bavarian grasslands

I think *I'm blind confounded*
my palate has claimed my tongue.

When Mercerdes Benz and Volkswagens
course silently through evening autobahns

I ask *how do I find my way to Odessa?*
Born burnt I can't mourn yet

what it means to be alive or dead
my cold embers won't light a flame

TO INNA

Burdened with sadness
you speak your beliefs
whatever the cost.
Frenzied then guilty
your eyes deaden
like unsilvered mirror

burn with the hot moist ash
of two histories, show
two ancient races' pain
and terror. In them
I've seen the taut mind
of a deep soul

ANTHEM

Derzhavin, your anthem has no place here
under ashy sky, on pulped grass.
The Virgin's icon lies splintered
in a pit of lime, as the enemy leaves us
to our confounded blink-eyed victory.
Lamb-dead, hut-vacant, camp-silent,
soldier-furrowed, soap-charred. Almighty
I'm afraid to go beyond the fields
vodka-glassed, victory-paraded
man-strong medalled.

A pregnant train is trailing its child.
I can't listen to an anthem gramophoned
by the wind. Mothers must make swaddling
for their girls, the balalaika must sing to me.

MOSES

The train of my black thought
tunnels through heaving sewers
races along all German, Soviet,
Polish roads and beyond.
Hurls through ovens, mortuaries,
ravages. All manner of death.

Then for the first time
God reveals his face to me
intact, spiritual, lit by the blaze
of gas inside the burning bush.

MIKHAEL

Can I call you in the garden
which hasn't changed since
that awful day? The same apples
ripen in the same endless sunshine.
But there's no phone to ring
and nothing's left of us there,
no laughter, no tears.
When I hear you speak to me now
you've not yet been ill, you're calm,
we're those penniless boys
who cross barefoot to the beach
as passing trams jangle by.

THE COSSACK WIFE

The school roof shines like mica,
moonlight soaks watermelons in the young grass,
windmill sails drone like jet engines.

A Cossack wife abandons her sewing to the dusk,
pins lie on the table, she stares at her mirror:
Is he being nursed or buried now?
It's been so long since he wrote from Voronezh.
The Commissar mumbles that the mail's delayed
then makes his clumsy pass at her.

Her leech-eyed mother-in-law lets herself in.
Oh please, full moon in the sky,
help the Cossack wife to love, to accept
to waste herself in tears.

STOPPED

Suddenly there's an elk caught
in our headlights. His gaze is dry,
his massive proportions overbearing,
his antlers giant like a shaman's headgear.

He is thoughtful not afraid knowing
not stunned. We're stopped on this forest path
100 kilometres from Moscow face to face
by the sadness in those eyes

I wish he'd escape and graze in darkness
let the starlight pierce the black coal of his stare,
but instead he stands transfixed by men
who cut the flesh they eat from live animals.

MOLDAVIAN IS A LANGUAGE

which hauls in the dark
until the last of sunset's banished
by its rugged horse and cart.

Can you hear the swagger,
of its coppery verbs,
the Latin of a convict's dagger
not the Senate's words?

The Capitol's heights have crumbled,
its artefacts lie low,
only the Dniester's windblown grumble
keeps the Roman known.

The songs of desperate outlaws
snipe at the words of the ruler,
clatter once they've stopped their chores
at night beyond Vorkuta.

To earn a bit more dinner
a puff of a cigarette,
the shivering political sinner
is singing aloud and yet

his Ovid is adapted here
crude but still astute,
don't segregate yourselves
for fear of thief or prostitute,

desperation makes us equal
as we sing and speak
we each contain the sequel
to the other's pique.

Mamalyga and wine at dawn
give courage to my gullet
and my words are more than brawn
as short lived as a bullet.

One day you'll all be literature
I've read The Almighty's Book,
that's why I had to come here
to know to listen to look.

ON A BLUE VASE

there's a July forest
with pines drawn in detail
and people in vague silhouette.

Thank God for the impetus
of this imprecise sketch
so brilliantly incomplete

GLOSSARY

Biblical Hebrew

Azzazel	page 19	scapegoat

Judaio Tajik

joma	page 13	ceremonial coat
ikat	page 13	pattern made by weaving individual silk thread, dyed in various colours
Jomi Hammam	page 18	hot coat
Bivi	page 18	grandma
corpa	page 18	eiderdown
rachmat koonah	page 19	R.I.P.
khundal	page 25	finest silk
Khon	page 25	the Emir, literally the Emir's finest silk
luvs	page 49	green marzipan topped with pistachios

Egyptian Arabic

oboule	page 49	at home
ghorayeba	page 49	ground almonds wrapped in icing sugared short crust pastry
conafa	page 49	pistachio wrapped in crispy shredded dough
halawa	page 49	halva

Irish

cabbeldy	page 52	makeshift

Moldavian

mamalyga	page 70	gruel

NOTES

DHIMMI page 20
Press reports in 2005 suggested young English Moslems polled both as wanting to live under Sharia Law and as not knowing what it was.

Dhimmi – a tenet of Sharia Law dating from the seventh century to the present which accords freedom of religion together with protection from persecution to Jews and Christians living from the Atlantic Ocean to Central Asia. *Dhimmi* status is granted in exchange for acceptance of Moslem supremacy to varying degrees which accord with the demands of the ruling sect. The italicised words are Judaio-Tajik.

BINYAMIN page 21
Binyamin Mammon – born circa 1808 in Boukhara.

LAG B'OMER page 53
Lag B'Omer – a day's break in the period of mourning between Passover and Pentacost.

ORIGINATING SUMMONS page 55
Written as poet in residence for Casa Shalom, an organization which helps Marranos (and others from families who secretly practiced Judaism after forced conversion) to establish their Jewish lineage, so they can obtain Israeli citizenship by invoking The Law of Return.

MOTHER ME ALWAYS page 57
Commissioned for the Mother's Day Celebration, St Nicholas Church, Idbury, Oxfordshire, Sunday 18th March 2007.

WITHOUT YOUR JEWS   page 59

Commissioned for reading in Bevis Marks Synagogue on the 16th December 2006, the concluding event of the 350th anniversary celebration of the re-admission of Jews to Britain. The law exiling them has never been repealed. The 300 year old synagogue (which is exclusively candle lit during the 25 hours of Sabbath and Festivals) has the longest history of unbroken worship in the Commonwealth.

CHARRED   page 62

Charred after Ashes (1967)

TO INNA (1979)   page 63

The poet Inna Lisnianskaya was Lipkin's wife. Her father was Jewish and her mother was Russian Orthodox.

ANTHEM   page 64

Anthem after Military Song (1981).

Derzhavin – 18th century poet who wrote military anthems commemorating Russian victories over the Ottomans.

MOSES (1967)   page 65

MIKHAEL   page 66

Mikhael after Brother (1996).

Mikhael – Semyon Lipkin's brother died in 1990.

THE COSSACK WIFE   page 67

The Cossack Wife after Cossack Woman (1942).

STOPPED   page 68

Stopped after Hostage (1960).

The Old Testament laws given to Noah for the civilization of mankind after the flood include a prohibition against eating flesh cut from live animals.

MOLDAVIAN IS A LANGUAGE (1962)   page 69

This is an example of a translation structured to prioritise rhyme scheme and scantion of the source text.

Vorkuta – town inside the arctic circle built by slave labour.

ON A BLUE VASE   page 70

On A Blue Vase (1974) after On a Blue Vessel.

The Author is indebted to Inna Lisnianskaya, Daniel Weissbort, Valentina Polukhina and Sveta Payne for their help with the Seymon Lipkin translations. Any deviations from their literal translations are her own.